I0144600

Amelia Earhart Was Married Here

Note from author: The following booklet about Amelia Earhart's wedding day (gleaned from interviewing the grandson of the judge who performed the ceremony), is an excerpt from my book, *Mystic Seafarer's Trail: Secrets behind the 7 Wonders,* Titanic's *Shoes, Captain Sisson's Gold, and Amelia Earhart's Wedding.* If you already purchased the *Mystic Seafarer's Trail*, you do not need to purchase this one.

Amelia Earhart Was Married Here

Little known details of Earhart's wedding in Noank, Connecticut

Lisa M. Saunders

Copyright © 2012 Lisa M. Saunders

All rights reserved.

ISBN-13: 978-0964940369 (Saunders Books)

ISBN-10: 0964940361

Image credits:
Cover photo Amelia Earhart plaque taken by Lisa Saunders
Headshot of Lisa Saunders by Cindy Barry
Photo of Church Street sign by Lisa Saunders
Photo of Lisa Saunders taken in front of Amelia Earhart plaque by Kate Poole

Lisa Saunders

CONTENTS

ACKNOWLEDGMENTS

Mary and Robert Anderson, Jr., of Noank, Connecticut, and Frank Reed of Conanicut Island, Rhode Island.

The following excerpt from the *Mystic Seafarer's Trail* gives you an idea of where the *Trail* will take you and Amelia Earhart's place on the trail:

1   WANTED: EPIC ADVENTURE

Shortly after stepping out of my new home with my hound for our first stroll through the historic seacoast village of Mystic, Connecticut, a woman pulled over in her van and yelled, "Excuse me."

Assuming she was a tourist wanting directions to Mystic Pizza or some other attraction, I wasn't prepared for what she really wanted to know.

"Do you realize the back of your skirt is tucked into your underwear?"

What a debut in my new hometown—I don't think this is what *National Geographic* meant when they named Mystic one of the top 100 adventure towns in the United States.

Once recovered from my wardrobe "malfunction," I continued toward downtown Mystic with Bailey, a beagle/basset hound mix, to embark on a new life and shake off my old, sedentary landlubbing ways.

No longer did I want to be known as the lady who always talks about losing weight but never does it. No longer would I sit around daydreaming about becoming thin and famous so I could hire someone else to clean my house. I had a real shot at it now that I lived in a place where I couldn't help but fall into a swash-buckling adventure—the kind that might inspire me to write a bestseller.

Straddling both sides of the Mystic River in the towns of Groton and Stonington, the village of Mystic takes its name from an Indian word, "river running to the sea." With its scenic views of tall ships, islands, lighthouses, and secluded coves, it has attracted such legendary honeymooners as Humphrey Bogart and Lauren Bacall. It is a place where those who cross the oceans gather to swap stories and repair their boats. It is where famous explorers are born, visit, get married, or come to live.

To launch my career as an adventuress, I decided to walk Bailey to the haunts and homes of such celebrated adventurers as Amelia Earhart, the first woman to fly solo across the Atlantic; Dr. Robert Ballard, the discoverer of *Titanic's* watery grave; Rear Admiral Richard E. Byrd, the first aviator to fly over the South Pole; and Captain Nathaniel B. Palmer, who accidentally discovered Antarctica.

Now was the time for me to join their ranks, to start living life on the edge. Maybe I could become thin and famous like Amelia Earhart. Like her, I am fairly tall, my middle initial is M, I have a gap between my two front teeth, and until I looked it up, I couldn't spell medieval either (more on that and her wedding day later). Unlike Amelia, I wasn't skinny, but that was about to change. I would stop lying around reading about adventurers and do what it took to become one.

My husband, Jim, and I were transferred to the Mystic area by his company, which meant I had to quit my job as a full-time writer for a college and search for a new one in a community revolving around life at sea—not easy for a confirmed desk sitter like me. Finding the area already teeming with underemployed writers and publicists, I was grateful when my former employer hired me back as a consulting writer. Although freelancing allowed me to work from home in my pajamas, it offered no retirement benefits—hence the need to become famous. Being famous not only helps pay the bills, but it gives you an edge when trying to accomplish other goals.

Now was the time for me to follow in the path of prominent authors such as Herman Melville who went to sea on a whaler (a ship designed to catch whales and process their oil) when he couldn't find a job. Although he deserted and had to live among cannibals for a time, he found the inspiration to write his first novel. Further sea adventures, which included mutiny and hearing about a whale that rammed and sank the *Essex*, led to the creation of his magnum opus: *Moby Dick*. I, myself, could barely get through this "Great American Novel," but somebody must like it. And now that I lived within walking distance of the *Charles W. Morgan*, the last wooden whaleship in the world, I felt that was a sign. Perhaps I could enlist on it as a deck swabber on some epic voyage. The house we purchased came with a brass, whale-shaped door knocker. That had to be a sign.

If following in the footsteps of a whaling writer didn't work, there was always the chance I could get famous by finding a dead body—just like Bailey and our older daughter had. Although it didn't make her into an international celebrity, I use it as a party stopper whenever I want to be the center of attention. Of course, I should really find my own body, preferably of a well-known person. Celebrities are always coming to Mystic to film movies or vacation.

Since I couldn't count on finding a dead body, famous or otherwise, I decided to start small. First, I planned to compile "The 7 Wonders of Mystic"—something quick I could shout to the tourists who rolled down their car windows asking what they should see (besides my underwear).

National Geographic's website suggests that Mystic adventurers bike what it calls the 25-mile Vineyard Loop that includes "some hairy climbs that stops at two of the best wineries." Hairy climbs? I hoped to get thin, but did I have to go uphill to do it? I thought not.

Instead, I would conquer a trail of my own design—one that would avoid hills where possible—and call it the "Mystic Seafarer's Trail." It would include "The 7 Wonders" (once I figured out what they were), plus the stomping grounds of legendary explorers. It would encompass the Mystic, Stonington and Noank area and even include where Kate the acupuncturist weighed her newborn on a lobster scale after giving birth on a schooner and rowing to shore.

With so many potential wonders to consider and adventures to try, I had a lot of ground—and water—to cover. So, every afternoon, I checked my skirt and off Bailey and I went to follow a scent of our own.

(THIS BOOKLET RESUMES WITH THE CHAPTER 11 EXCERPT OF THE *MYSTIC SEAFARER'S TRAIL*.)

11 AMELIA EARHART WAS MARRIED HERE—A "DEEP, DARK SECRET"

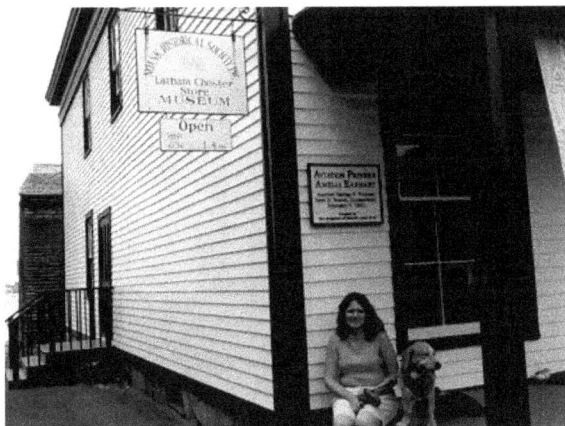

One day in the summer of 2011, Bailey and I left our house on Allyn Street in Mystic, Connecticut, and walked straight down to West Mystic Avenue. Making a right on Noank Road, we strolled to the quint, little fishing village of Noank.

I was meeting seafaring friend Kate there so I could film her in front of Ford's Lobster shack (seen in the movie, *Mystic Pizza*) where she weighed her baby after giving birth to her on a schooner on September 15, 1984, and rowing to shore.[i]

When I was done filming Kate, she and I walked over to the Noank Historical Society's Latham/Chester Store, located between a public beach and an oyster farming business. Kate filmed me in front of the plaque attached to the Latham/Chester Store that states, "Aviation Pioneer Amelia Earhart married George P. Putnam here in Noank, Connecticut, February 7, 1931." I assumed that the words, "here in Noank," meant that she got married in that building, so that is what I said on the video I uploaded to YouTube that very day.

Months later, while eating my breakfast at Carson's Variety Store, a tiny spot where Noank locals have been gathering for a century, I asked the woman sipping her coffee on the stool next to mine what she knew about Earhart's wedding at the Latham/Chester Store.

To my horror, she replied, "She didn't get married there, she got married around the corner on Church Street, in the house that once belonged to my great-grandfather, John McDonald. I don't know what

5

happened with the property after he died on July 17, 1911. I am assuming my great-grandmother lived there until her death. At the time of Amelia Earhart's wedding, it belonged to George Putnam's mother."

Mary Anderson, Curator of the Noank Historical Society, confirmed what my breakfast companion Barbara Servidio told me—that Earhart was indeed secretly married in a simple civil ceremony in the square, flat-roofed house I found on Church Street. (A deed I found at Groton Town Hall confirmed that Mrs. Putnam purchased the house from the estate of Barbara's great-grandfather in 1930.)

Learning I was including this information in a book about the area, Mary said, "You tell everybody that the wedding scene portrayed in the movie [*Amelia*] is inaccurate. My husband's grandfather, the Groton probate judge, performed the ceremony, and my father-in-law, Robert Anderson, a young Noank lawyer at the time, attended as a witness. Before and after the ceremony, Amelia spoke to him about a new kind of aircraft she was promoting. When the judge congratulated her after the ceremony, calling her Mrs. Putnam, she replied, 'Please sir, I prefer Miss Earhart.'"

Most accounts of Earhart's life barely mention her wedding at all, except to say she got married—reluctantly. The 2009 movie *Amelia* starring Hilary Swank showed her getting married outside—despite the early February date.

I was determined to learn the truth behind this historic event. Mary's comment about Earhart rejecting the name, "Mrs. Putnam," was quickly confirmed. When *The New York Times* announced her wedding the following day, its front-page headline read:

Amelia Earhart Weds G.P. Putnam
But Atlantic Flier Will Remain 'Miss Earhart' for Business Purposes and Writing

To get a better idea of what Noank residents and two black cats experienced the day of the wedding, Mary walked me over to a wide, low cabinet under a display case at the Historical Society's Sylvan Street Museum. Pulling out the drawer containing E's, she handed me the Earhart file full of old newspaper clippings and eye-witness accounts of the secret wedding. This folder was a goldmine—especially the manuscript, "Amelia Earhart in Noank," written by Mary's husband, Noank Attorney Robert Anderson, Jr.

Robert Anderson, Jr., stated in his manuscript that his family became involved with the Putnams when George Putnam's widowed mother, Frances B. Putnam, was looking to buy a summer home near her friend, artist Katherine "Speedy" Forest, in Noank. "My father, then 24 years old and one year out of law school, represented her in the purchase negotiations…To the best of my knowledge she hired him because he was then the only lawyer in Noank."[ii]

When Frances Putnam tried to help her son arrange a private wedding to Amelia in Noank, she contacted the lawyer who handled the purchase of her house. Robert Anderson, Jr., stated, "In preparation for her son's hoped-for marriage to Amelia, Mrs. Putnam asked my father to arrange for a Justice-of-the Peace to perform a small, private ceremony in her home. Not being one to miss such an opportunity, my father volunteered his father, Arthur P. Anderson, who was Groton's Judge of Probate and as such could perform the marriage."

According to the history books, Earhart, originally from Atchison, Kansas, was a "reluctant bride," having refused Putnam's marriage proposals six times. She met Putnam, an arctic explorer, publicist and heir to the GP Putnam publishing company, in 1928 while employed as a social worker in Boston. George Putnam had become famous as the publisher of Charles Lindbergh's book about his solo flight across the Atlantic in 1927. Now George Putnam was helping sponsors look for a woman to become the first woman to fly the Atlantic in the trimotor Fokker, *Friendship*, previously owned by pioneering aviator and polar explorer, Richard E. Byrd. Amelia was interviewed by the flight sponsors in New York City at the offices of G.P. Putnam's Sons Publishing Company. Upon concluding the interview in George Putnam's office, George accompanied Amelia to the train station. Shortly after returning to Boston, she received the offer to make the historic flight.

Although Earhart didn't touch the controls in her transatlantic flight with two male pilots in 1928, she nonetheless received a ticker tape parade in New York as the first woman to make it across the Atlantic by air. She found it embarrassing to receive so much fanfare when she said she felt about as useful as a sack of potatoes on the trip.

Despite her feelings about her role on that flight, she moved into George Putnam's home in Rye, New York, and wrote a book about her experiences. In the process, she became a close friend of George's wife, Dorothy, and their two sons, George Jr. and David. After her book, *20 Hours 40 Minutes*, was completed, Amelia dedicated it to her friend Dorothy Binney Putnam.

In December of 1929, Dorothy divorced George Putnam in Reno, Nevada, citing "failure to provide" and remarried the following month (she would remarry two more times).[iii]

Putnam, who was reportedly smitten by Amelia, brought Earhart to Noank to visit with his mother, Frances Putnam, and on November 8, 1930, he convinced Amelia to visit Groton Town Hall to apply for a marriage license.

Wanting to follow Amelia's trail, I visited Groton Town Hall to see if I could learn anything from looking at the license. Just before I entered the building, a friendly, owner-less golden retriever greeted me. Calling the phone number etched in his tag, I assured the owner I would hold onto him until she could drive over to collect him.

As I sat on a bench with the dog at the entrance of the 1908 brick building, I pondered what Earhart was thinking before she stepped through that doorway more than 80 years earlier. My first trip to Groton Town Hall occurred two years ago when we first moved to Mystic. It wasn't for any life-altering reason—I was just required by law to register Bailey for a Connecticut dog license.

Amelia, on the other hand, was apparently extremely apprehensive when she entered Groton Town Hall. She wasn't sold on the idea of marriage in general (her parents had divorced six years earlier in 1924) [iv] and had rejected other marriage proposals, including Sam Chapman's, whose proposal included the insistence that his wife not work outside the home.

According to Amelia's friends, she felt an additional reluctance to marry George Putnam because she had become friends with his first wife, Dorothy. According to author Susan Butler, Earhart was unhappy to think Putnam's feelings for her were a cause of their divorce.[v] Although Dorothy was already remarried, her divorce from Putnam was less than a year old.

Once freed from my dog sitting responsibilities, I visited the Registrar of Vital Statistics office, the same office where I applied for Bailey's dog license.

When I told the clerk I was looking for Earhart's marriage license and gave her the wedding date, she found it immediately. "We've had many requests for that," she said. She handed me the book containing the original license so I could decide if I wanted to pay the $20 for a certified copy of it. I touched Amelia's signature, hoping that some of her adventurous spirit would rub off on me. Wanting extra insurance that it would, I purchased a certified, first generation copy of it with a raised seal. Now I had certified proof that Amelia could tell a lie—she listed herself as 32, a year younger than she really was at 33. According to authors Elgen M. and Marie K. Long, this deception began on a May 1923 aviator pilot certificate that stated she was born on July 24, 1898.[vi] She was actually born on July 24, 1897. For whatever reason, she continued to give the public, including Groton Town Hall, that younger age.

At the time Earhart and Putnam applied for the wedding license, Connecticut law required a five-day waiting period from the application to the wedding. On the back of the marriage license, a typed statement from Probate Court was attached (misspelling Earhart's last name, a handwritten "a" was inserted after the "e") granting the couple permission to celebrate the intended marriage "without delay." Nevertheless, Earhart did delay.

William, the youngest son of Probate Judge Arthur Anderson, recalled his impression of the reluctant bride in a 1989 article by Larry Chick: *"Amelia and George came to see my father at his house at the corner of Brook and Elm. They wanted to talk to him about the possibility of his marrying them, and I was the teenager in the way who was shooed into another room to give them some privacy. But even in the next room I heard her ask my father if she could go into his study and have a cigarette and think about marriage. When she came out, she had decided against it."[vii]*

According to the 2009 *Amelia* movie and other sources, Earhart didn't smoke and was criticized for promoting Lucky Strike cigarettes on her first trip across the Atlantic (smoking wasn't considered ladylike). Isn't it just like a little brother to tell on you for smoking—whether you did or not?

Promoting cigarettes gave Earhart a continued connection to Rear-Admiral Richard E. Byrd, the polar explorer who previously owned the Fokker she used on her first transatlantic flight. Byrd had also came to the Mystic area when he visited the Nathanial B. Palmer House in Stonington to study Palmer's notes on the Antarctic in preparation for his history-making flight over the South Pole on November 29, 1929. (According to Mary Beth Baker, Director of the Stonington Historical Society, "He [Byrd] wanted to review the logbooks, journals, charts, and letters that had accumulated over the years in the family home." According to research by Palmer House's first curator, Constance Colom, "It was at Byrd's suggestion that the family donated *Hero's* logbook to the Library of Congress in the 1930s."[viii])

Earhart had gotten to know Byrd and his wife in Boston while preparing for her flight across the Atlantic in his former plane.[ix] Byrd served as a technical consultant for the trip.[x] Less than two months after her successful flight, Earhart contributed financially to Byrd's flight over the South Pole. On July 30, 1928, she sent a letter to Byrd at the Biltmore Hotel in New York (letter online at Ohio State University Libraries) stating, *"Perhaps you noticed my 'endorsement' of a kind of cigarettes which were carried by the men in the plane. I made this deliberately. It made possible my offering a modest contribution to your Antarctic expedition, which otherwise I could not have done."[xi]*

When Earhart supposedly smoked a cigarette in Judge Anderson's study and came out deciding against marriage for the moment, Robert Anderson recalled her mood in a 1976 article by reporter Jeff Mill. *"Amelia was a little bit subdued. She just wanted to think about the whole thing more. She had dedicated herself to the business of flying, and she was anxious to retain her individuality. She was very devoted to George, there's no doubt about that. But she was afraid that changing her name somehow would diminish her stature, and she was a little upset about it."* Robert added that George Putnam *"was very considerate about it."*[xii]

When the media learned that no wedding occurred upon taking out the wedding license, it fell to Robert Anderson, as Mrs. Putnam's lawyer and friend, to tell reporters that the wedding had been delayed, not cancelled.

Three months later, on Friday, February 6, 1931, George Putnam called his mother and told her he and Amelia would be secretly driving out from New York to Noank that night. They would marry the following day, February 7 (the *Titanic* couple I featured in the *Mystic Seafarer's Trail*, the Smiths, also got married on a February 7—perhaps this is not a good wedding date for those planning a trip across an ocean?).

Very few knew that Earhart and Putnam had come to Noank, but resident Clifford Sullivan, approximately 12 at the time, stated in the 1976 Mill article that when he heard the news that "Lady Lindy" was in town, it was *"like trying to get into the Kennedy compound in Hyannis..."* He and his friends rode up and down the street on their bicycles, *"trying to get a peek of, you know, Amelia Earhart."*[xiii]

When reporters caught wind of what was going on, Robert Anderson's younger brother Ashby got his chance to participate in the historic event. Repeatedly calling the judge's home, the reporters wanted details on the couple's plans. According to the article by Chick, Ashby and his brothers avoided giving them any answers by telling them they had to call the judge's secretary to get that kind of information.[xiv]

On the day of the wedding, Putnam received a typed letter, or some would say contract, from Amelia. I read a copy of her handwritten draft (available online at Purdue University Libraries), which is just slightly different than the typed one he received (the handwritten draft was done on stationery I presume was Mrs. Putnam's, and included cross-outs and insertions as Amelia fine-tuned what she wanted to say). The stationary didn't have an exact address for George Putnam's home, but it was printed with the following in all capitals:

PHONE MYSTIC 1016
TELEPHONE NOANK
NOANK, CONNECTICUT
THE SQUARE HOUSE
CHURCH STREET

The following are excerpts from Amelia's handwritten version:

...You must know again my reluctance to marry, my feeling that I shatter thereby chances in work which means most to me...

On our life together I want you to understand I shall not hold you to any midaevil [Earhart's misspelling, not mine!] *code of faithfulness to me nor shall I consider myself so bound to you. If we can be honest about affection for others which may come to [either] of us the difficulties of such situations may be avoided...*

I must exact a cruel promise and that is you will let me go in a year if we find no happiness together...[xv]

Just prior to the noon wedding, Amelia sat speaking to Robert Anderson, who was serving as a witness, on a couch in a small sitting room in the back of the yellow house. There were no special wedding decorations, not even flowers.

"She was completely wrapped up in the aviation business," Anderson said.[xvi] The groom, his mother, and his uncle, were also in the room.

Amelia told Robert about her desire to interest the Army and Navy in the military potential of the autogyro, a precursor to the helicopter. Robert Anderson, Jr., recalled what his father told him about that conversation: "Although the Navy representatives were considerably more receptive than their Army counterparts, you can just imagine how unwelcome this advice was to the generals and admirals she visited, and she was treated accordingly. Even at her wedding she was still steaming at their repudiation of her. Pa let her talk, just to get the anger out of her system. But no such thing. My grandfather and George summoned Amelia to step forward for the five-minute ceremony (totally secular and omitting all mention of "obedience"), and almost reluctantly she went over to be married."[xvii]

The men wore business attire and Amelia wore a brown traveling suit, light brown blouse, shoes and stockings. Robert Anderson said that she was *"a much more attractive individual as a young woman than she was depicted...she was quite delicate looking with beautiful color and light brown hair—all in all, very attractive."* Robert recalled that it was *"quite obvious that she had become satisfied that she did want to go through with it* [the wedding]."[xviii]

Although *The New York Times* stated that the ceremony took place in the living room while a "crackling fire burned in the fireplace," Robert Anderson remembered that his father (the judge) stood in the dining room, Earhart and Putnam stood in the passageway between the sitting room and dining room, and behind them stood George's mother and himself. Wherever the ceremony took place, all agree it was over in less than five minutes. Robert said, *"They both wanted it that way, so my father did little more than bring out the essentials of the marriage contract."*[xix]

The New York Times added: *"As Mr. Putnam slipped a plain platinum ring on*

Miss Earhart's finger the cats, coal black and playful, rubbed arched backs against his ankles."[xx]

After the ceremony, Earhart and Robert returned to the sofa. Where, according to Robert Anderson, Jr., Amelia "resumed her diatribe against those stuffed shirts in the War Department."

George's mother came over to them, placed a set of amber beads around Amelia's neck and leaned down to kiss her.[xxi] Preparing to leave, Judge Anderson came forward to congratulate everyone, addressing Amelia as "Mrs. Putnam."

Amelia replied, "Please, sir, I prefer Miss Earhart."

According to Robert Anderson, Jr. during our phone interview, his grandfather was unaccustomed to such "modern" airs. "My grandfather drew himself up to his full 5 feet, 8 inches, and barked, 'That service was short but effective.'"[xxii] With that, he left.

George Putnam called his secretary in New York to announce the wedding. There was no reception or honeymoon, and the couple was back at their desks on Monday.

The New York Times described Noank as a "quaint little village," one that "dozes" in the winter. In regard to the wedding, most of the residents were "asleep," having no idea what had just taken place. One recalled the event as a "deep, dark secret."[xxiii]

Another said, "It was all very hush-hush. I don't think the people next-door even knew about it."[xxiv]

According to comments from Noank's Historian, Mary Virginia Goodman, residents "wouldn't go all to pieces about this sort of thing" and described the couple as "outlanders invading our little village."[xxv] Despite Goodman's opinion of the "outlanders," she did accommodate the request made by phone to her home the following day. She was asked if she could provide a picture of the house where Earhart had married and send it to a business in New York that sold photographs to newspapers. To fulfill this assignment, Goodman said she "obtained the services of Moses W. Rathbun, the village postmaster at the time, who was also very good with a camera…" Goodman took the roll of film, along with a photograph of Judge Anderson, which he provided, and rode the trolley to New London, Connecticut. From there, she sent the images by express to New York.[xxvi]

When interviewed by the *New York Times* about the wedding shortly afterwards, George's mother confirmed there had been no fuss, no flowers, and the neighbors had not been notified. When the subject of flying came up, she said she had never been, and although she was afraid, she intended to fly with her daughter-in-law soon. Amelia had promised her, "I'll take you for a ride the next time I come up here."

"I'll not be afraid with her," Frances Putnam told the interviewer.[xxvii]

Apparently, Earhart was happy enough in her marriage to Putnam. That

Christmas, they sent Judge Anderson a card with a caricature of themselves flying together in an autogyro, which, in the sketch, looks like a small, open cockpit airplane with a propeller attached to its nose and a large one on top. A giant Santa is holding the autogyro in the air. Underneath Santa, it states:

Happy Landings!
G.P.P
A.E.[xxviii]

Putnam and Earhart continued to plan and promote her flying projects after their marriage. A few months after the wedding, Amelia set a world altitude record in an autogyro;[xxix] and in 1932, she became the first woman to fly solo nonstop across the Atlantic—a trip fraught with weather and mechanical problems. Her Lockheed Vega even went into a spin, sending her toward "whitecaps too close for comfort."[xxx]

In 1936, Earhart began planning a round-the-world flight, intending to take the long, dangerous route near the equator—despite the fact that several pilots had died in the attempt. Earhart's last, legendary flight occurred in a specially modified Lockheed Electra 10E, which she dubbed the "flying laboratory."

On July 2, 1937, Earhart and her navigator, Fred Noonan, disappeared somewhere over the Pacific Ocean. They were unable to find Howland Island, where they were scheduled to land for refueling. Among her last words reported to the Coast Guard cutter, *Itasca,* were: "We must be on you, but cannot see you—but gas is running low. Have been unable to reach you by radio. We are flying at 1,000 feet."

After an extensive, expensive search failed to find Earhart, Noonan, and the Lockheed Electra, the government abandoned its search on July 18. George Putnam financed his own search until October 1937.[xxxi]

Putnam publicly released a letter Earhart had given him in the event one of her flights ended in tragedy: *"Please know that I am quite aware of the hazards. I want to do it—because I want to do it. Women must try to do things as men have tried. When they fail, their failure must be but a challenge to others."*[xxxii]

A year and a half after her disappearance, on January 5, 1939, Putnam had her declared legally dead—way ahead of the required seven-year waiting period. He remarried that same year, but was divorced in 1944, and remarried again. He died January 4, 1950, in California.

The home Earhart and Putnam were married in is now a privately owned duplex. According to a 1979 article by reporter Steve Fagin, the owner celebrated her wedding anniversary annually with his friends. In her honor, they've raised their glasses to her and sung, "For She's a Jolly Good Fellow."[xxxiii]

In June of 2010, NavList, a community of celestial navigation enthusiasts, wanted the public to know that Earhart had a very personal connection to Noank so donated the sign I found attached to the Noank Historical Society's Latham/Chester Store. Frank Reed, manager of NavList, believed Earhart's flying companion, Fred Noonan, was a top navigator. In a 2010 article by Matt Collette, Reed said, "[Noonan] *was the sort of person who knew how to get across oceans precisely, accurately...But a few clouds could ruin their day, and that's very well what could have happened.*"[xxxiv]

Although most of the world believes Amelia simply ran out of fuel over the Pacific Ocean near Howland Island, the possibility that her plane landed on a reef off the remote Pacific island of Nikumaroro is currently under investigation by The International Group for Historic Airplane Recovery (TIGHAR). A statement from their website: *"A review of high-definition underwater video footage taken during the recently-completed Niku VII expedition has revealed a scattering of man-made objects on the reef slope off the west end of Nikumaroro. The newly discovered debris field is in deep water offshore the location where an object thought to be Lockheed Electra landing gear appears in a photo taken three months after Amelia Earhart disappeared. Items in the debris field appear to be consistent with the object in the 1937 photo.*"[xxxv]

In 1940, a partial skeleton of a woman matching Earhart's size and race, plus a jar the shape of an anti-freckle cream available in the 30s, was found in the remains of a campfire under a tree on the island of Nikumaroro (Earhart was known to dislike her freckles). Had Earhart used that jar to boil water? The heel and partial sole of a woman's shoe manufactured in the 1930s, plus a box used to hold a nautical sextant (a navigational tool) were also found. Did Earhart and Noonan die as castaways? If so, how long did they struggle to stay alive, hoping for rescue?

In a 2012 article by Malia Mattoch McManus, fish and bird bones were also found[xxxvi] suggesting someone might have been marooned for months.

(Note to self: If I ever find a friend with a sailboat, I must learn celestial navigation, how to use a GPS—and how to catch fish!)

(THIS BOOKLET RESUMES WITH AN EXCERPT FROM CHAPTER 14 OF THE *MYSTIC SEAFARER'S TRAIL.*)

14 SHANGHAIED PART II

In an effort to make sailing preparations for our winter trip up the east coast more fun, Jules decided Jim and I could have our own titles. Though blind, she was the most experienced sailor and would be making all the sailing decisions. Having named their 33' sloop *Watercolors* in honor of her passion for art, she went on to declare herself the Sailing Master; Neil (her fiancé), Captain; Jim, Skipper; and me, Navigator. I was pleased with Navigator, especially since I had recently learned how to locate the North Star. No matter what time of night or time of year, it stays in virtually the same position, making it an ideal tool for celestial navigation (unless, of course, it's a cloudy night).

And yet, maybe I didn't want that title. Although it sounded more impressive than deck-swabber, everyone blames the navigator, not the deck-swabber, when voyages go awry—as in Amelia Earhart's disappearance when her navigator, Fred Noonan, was unable to locate Howland Island.

To tell the truth, although I *knew* how to find the North Star, actually finding it was a very different matter. For such an important star, the North Star isn't very bright and shiny. Located at the end of the little dipper, you'd think it would be easy to spot, but even the little dipper can be allusive at times (it's near the bowl part of the big dipper). Plus, there would be a whole lot more to learn than the North Star if I really wanted to help with navigation. But did I really need to bother since Jules and Neil had GPS (Global Positioning System), the satellite navigation system?

When I asked a seasoned world sailor why he took the trouble to continually study celestial navigation given the capabilities of GPS, he replied, "Are you kidding me? Every sailor, especially those who travel off shore, should learn celestial navigation. You need battery power to operate a GPS. What if the battery on the boat dies?"

When I wrote to Frank Reed, NavList manager and celestial navigation instructor, about the necessity of learning celestial navigation as a backup for GPS, he wrote back:

Well, as for GPS, I'll tell you what I tell everybody: the best backup for a GPS is another GPS (carefully stowed in a metal case with spare batteries replaced before every trip out of sight of land). Celestial navigation can be a worthwhile "backup of last resort," but it's no replacement for GPS. GPS has many advantages over traditional celestial navigation:

1) GPS is more accurate by a factor of 100. That's enough to steer around local hazards and operate in hazardous waters even with zero visibility. By contrast, celestial navigation only provides a position fix accurate to a mile or two and must be supplemented with other navigational methods when close to shore.

2) GPS provides a nearly continuous position plot. There's no need to extrapolate from your last fix. It's always "live."

3) GPS is easy. A child can understand it in five minutes.

4) GPS can be, and usually is, incorporated into a complete charting solution. The customizable displays of modern GPS "systems" include charts and can include built-in hazard avoidance intelligence and displays of other vessels' positions, too (have you seen marinetraffic.com? It's fun for identifying and tracking larger vessels off southern New England).

5) THE BIG ONE: GPS is all-weather. You can use it in the middle of a hurricane. By contrast, a few clouds or simply a hazy horizon can render celestial navigation useless for days at a time.

Of course, GPS does have some disadvantages, and these require learning and adapting to some modern issues. The biggest issue, of course, is power failure. If a full GPS "system" goes down, you lose many of the advantages I listed above. If you have a backup, handheld GPS, you will know exactly where you are in terms of latitude and longitude, which is great. But where is home? A modern navigator needs a set of latitude/longitude waypoints, written down on some waterproof material that can at least get you back to a safe port by following the readout of a basic handheld GPS. And of course, batteries—lots and lots of batteries, for the backup device.

So why bother with celestial navigation at all? First, there are non-essential reasons that have a lot of merit: it's a mark of a true mariner, it's a link to a great historical tradition of navigation, and it's good, clean fun. For practical navigation, it's one of those things that you might never use in a lifetime, but if that day arrives when all the electronics are out, and someone forgot to buy batteries, but just by chance you remembered to buy the Nautical Almanac for the current year, then the stars can get you across an ocean just as easily as they did 150 years ago. And many mariners still enjoy it because it provides that assurance of independence—the confidence that you won't need to call for help and put someone else's life at risk just because you forgot to buy batteries. From my perspective, that's the best practical reason for learning celestial navigation."

Frank Reed
Conanicut Island, Rhode Island

(For more information about NavList, an online community devoted to the preservation and practice of celestial navigation and other methods of traditional position-finding, visit www.fer3.com/arc, or contact Frank Reed at Frank@ReedNavigation.com.)

The following is more about *Mystic Seafarer's Trail* in case you would like to read the whole story that includes Amelia Earhart's place on the trail.

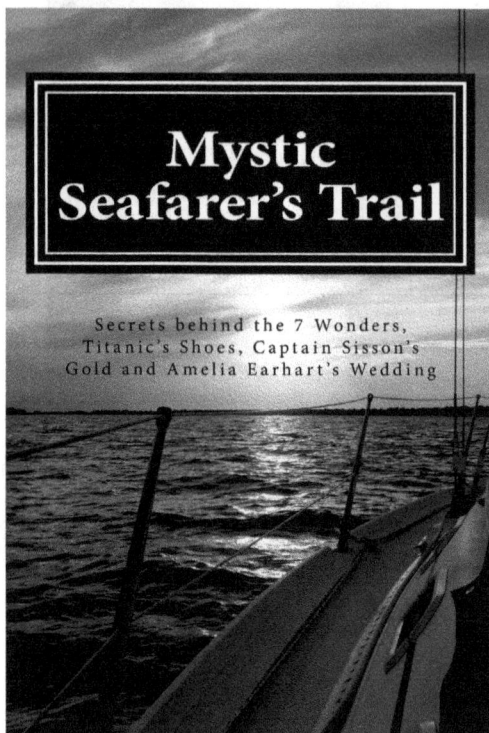

Mystic Seafarer's Trail

Secrets behind the 7 Wonders, Titanic's Shoes, Captain Sisson's Gold and Amelia Earhart's Wedding

Mystic Seafarer's Trail takes a humorous and historical look at the haunts and homes of Mystic's famous sea voyagers--living and dead. While searching for the Seven Wonders of Mystic with her beagle/basset hound, author Lisa Saunders uncovers the secrets behind the *Titanic's* shoes, Captain Sisson's hunt for gold, and Amelia Earhart's Noank wedding. But will she ever find an adventure of her own—one that will make her thin and famous? When walking the Mystic Seafarer's Trail (which Lisa designed for those who don't like to go uphill), she meets a blind sailor who invites her on a long, winter voyage. Can this landlubber defy squalls, scurvy, and her fear of scraping barnacles to survive this epic journey?

What people are saying about *Mystic Seafarer's Trail*:

"You will laugh out loud at Lisa's adventures in this part travel guide, part historical reference and completely hilarious tale."
Bree Shirvell, Editor, Stonington-Mystic Patch

"Lisa Saunders has written an engaging and solidly researched narrative which should capture the attention of all who are interested in early New England history and the traditions of the sea that were one of its foundations."
David S. Martin, Ph.D., Professor/Dean Emeritus, Gallaudet University, Washington, DC

"Entertaining, witty, informative—and cute! It covers a range of topics from personal loss to finding life, history and new friends."
Kristin Hartnett, Executive Director, Laughworks, Mystic, Connecticut

"I laughed out loud on a number of occasions. It's interesting, humorous and touching."
Glenn Gordinier, author of "Surfing Cold Water: A New Englander's Off-Season Obsession"

"This book is a splendid way to tie Mystic's history to life today—a bridge from the past to the present—for any age." Lou Allyn, Masons Island[xxxvii]

"An historical—and sometimes hysterical—look at Mystic. I can't wait to visit!"
Marianne Greiner, Illustrator, New York

"I found Lisa's anticipation of her sailing adventure just plain entertaining and could relate to her internal dialogue, misgivings, and somewhat grandiose fantasies. She is a person worth spending time with."
Ann Kuehner, Licensed Clinical Social Worker, New York

To purchase the *Mystic Seafarer's Trail*, available as both an e-book or softcover (the softcover version includes an index), visit Lisa's website at www.authorlisasaunders.com

ABOUT THE AUTHOR

Lisa Saunders is an award-winning writer and speaker living in Mystic, Connecticut, with her husband and hound. She works as a part-time history interpreter at Mystic Seaport and is a member of the Mystic River Historical Society. A graduate of Cornell University, she is the author of several books and a winner of the National Council for Marketing & Public Relations Gold Medallion. She is the Congenital CMV Foundation parent representative working to prevent the leading viral cause of birth defects—congenital cytomegalovirus.

OTHER BOOKS BY LISA SAUNDERS

EVER TRUE: A UNION PRIVATE AND HIS WIFE

The Civil War love letters of a Union Private and his 17-year-old wife. Published by Heritage Books.

Reviews:

"The story of how the marriage between Charles and Nancy survives separation, disease, the threat of death, and malicious gossip is compelling."
Pamela Goddard, Ithaca Times

"I was thoroughly fascinated by the letters and much impressed by the artful way the material was woven together. The story is cohesive and informative, but charming and romantic in a very personal way - I think this has real potential on several different fronts." Corinne Will, Managing Editor, Heritage Books, Inc.

Excerpt from introduction: I carefully unfolded the stiff yellowed paper, incredulous that I was actually touching a letter written during the American Civil War. It was one of 150 letters written between my great-great grandparents that I had discovered in a small wooden box in my mother's attic in Suffern, New York. The note I held in my hand, authored by Private Charles McDowell to his wife Nancy, was written on a small, plain piece of stationery--not at all fancy like some of the others in the batch which bore sketches of the White House and battle engagements. I gently smoothed it flat on the table, afraid I would tear it. The handwriting was strange, the ink somewhat faded, making it difficult to read. And then suddenly I came upon a word I recognized in an instant--Abe! It read, "We have [Secretary of State] Seward down here about every other day, and sometimes he fetches Old Abe with him and [he] looks about like any old farmer." I couldn't believe it - Charles met Lincoln!

In addition to the letters was Nancy's obituary, which reads: "MRS. MCDOWELL IS DEAD - SHOOK HANDS WITH LINCOLN. With the death of Mrs. Nancy Wager McDowell...the town of Sodus probably loses the distinction of having a resident who could boast of having shaken hands and talked with the martyred Lincoln... Mr. McDowell was a member of the Ninth New York Heavy Artillery in the Union Army and it was while stationed near Washington that his wife had an opportunity to speak with the President. Mrs. McDowell passed nearly a year in that vicinity and many were the pies she baked for the soldiers stationed at the capital. Typhoid Fever caused her to return to Alton to the home of her parents..." ("The Record," Sodus, Wayne County, N.Y. September 18, 1931)

I took the collection of letters back to my home in Maryland and began what was to become an exciting ten-year adventure. First I arranged the letters from Charles by date and began to read. Once I grew accustomed to his old-style handwriting and run-on sentences, I felt myself leaving the present and entering his past. I traveled back over 130 years and joined Charles in heart and mind. I felt his loneliness, his boredom, his fear. I laughed when he found a reason to laugh. He and his brother had enlisted despite his Canadian father's pleas to stay out of the war. As the months of his service turned into years, I hurt over his deep longing for his wife and home and for the life and family he left behind in Canada.

In other letters I was shocked to read of the desertions, hangings, amputations, prostitution, and even theft and murder among Union troops. Charles wrote home about the battles of Cold Harbor, Jerusalem Plank Road, Monocacy, Opequon (Winchester), Cedar Creek, the Siege of Petersburg, an attack by Mosby's Men, and the Shenandoah Valley Campaign.

Next I tackled Nancy's writing. As her collection of letters drew to an end, I was completely immersed in her anxious thoughts about Charles's welfare. She hoped there hadn't been a "ball made to kill" him. She hoped he wouldn't get too close to the Southern women when he occupied their homes. She longed for him to return to her--even if it was just for a short furlough. She wrote that she would rather be dead than continue to live the way they were. I now pondered the final years of her life spent rocking in her chair looking out the window. Perhaps she was awaiting her death so Charles could come for her once more...

To buy Ever True: 1-800-876-6103 or visit:
www.authorlisasaunders.com

SHAYS' REBELLION:
The Hanging of Co-Leader, Captain Henry Gale

Lisa's ancestor, a Revolutionary War veteran, is found guilty of treason and sentenced to be hanged for his leadership role in Shays' Rebellion. Visit www.authorlisasaunders.com for more information.

ANYTHING BUT A DOG!
The perfect pet for a girl with congenital CMV (cytomegalovirus)

The true story of a big, homeless canine and the little girl who needed him.

Reviews:

"Saunders takes readers on a road trip as harrowing as any Dog Whisperer training challenge...Beyond the laughs about a dizzying pet search, Saunders' dog tale is about a mother who candidly reveals her family's burden, love, and acceptance of a daughter born with severe disabilities-and the people, and pets, forever touched by her life."
Tonia Shakespeare, Rockland Magazine

"Sheds light on a disorder that is preventable and not talked about enough. If you're an animal lover, you'll love the critter tales as much as the special-needs storyline...really lifted my spirits." Terri Mauro, About.com

Anything But a Dog! is available through the author's website at www.authorlisasaunders.com and through the National CMV Disease Registry at: www.unlimitedpublishing.com/cmv (If purchased through the CMV Registry, a portion of the proceeds is donated to CMV research and parent support.)
Publisher at: http://www.unlimitedpublishing.com/saunders

RIDE A HORSE, NOT AN ELEVATOR

Lisa leaves the bullies and elevators of New York City to confront the outhouses, horses and eccentric relatives on her grandparents' farm. Chosen by Cornell University for its "Horse Book in a Bucket" program. Review:

"A 'warm fuzzy' in paperback form. It is a tangible tale for storytelling that provides a springboard for discussion between children and adults." Ruth Zwick, Educational Director, Sentinel Publications

Ride a Horse, Not an Elevator, is a children's novel about a test of young courage. In this story, based on Lisa's childhood summers, Lisa is a chubby city girl searching for friendship and excitement. She leaves home, and the elevators and bullies of a big apartment complex, to spend a summer in the country at her grandparents' farm. Culture shock! Accompanied only by her loyal beagle, Donald Dog, Lisa faces a summer in a very different environment with its own challenges and dangers. Using an outhouse is the least of her problems! She is terrified of her new pony. Lisa's grandfather is injured by a charging cow and needs her to ride the pony to get help. Remembering Grandma's lesson about how love overcomes fear, she pushes herself past her anxieties to ride alone and obtain the help he needs. The book includes recipes from grandma's kitchen.

LISA'S FREE E-BOOKS

Visit Lisa's website at: www.authorlisasaunders.com to download the following free e-books:

How to Get Published
How to Get a Job
How to Promote Your Business (or yourself)

LISA'S SPEAKING TOPICS INCLUDE:

1. Graveyard Adventures—you never know who you will meet!
2. The Hanging of Henry Gale—from patriot to traitor in Shays' Rebellion
3. The 7 Wonders of Mystic
4. Finding Humor on Life's Adventures—and Misadventures!
5. Civil War: Union Private & His Wife (available as a talk, one-act play, or combination)
6. How to Get Published
7. How to Get a Job (Lisa is a former employment recruiter)
8. Stop CMV (Lisa is the Congenital CMV Foundation parent representative)
9. How to Get Free Publicity
10. Children's Writing Workshop (Cornell University included *Ride a Horse, Not an Elevator* in its "Horse Book in a Bucket" program)
11. A Time to Weep, A Time to Laugh—Moving forward after the death of a child

Lisa's appearances: USA 9 News… Cornell University… West Point Museum…Washington Independent Writers Association… Centers for Disease Control and Prevention (CDC)… Seward House… Lincoln Depot Museum…Johns Hopkins University… Siemens Healthcare Diagnostics… Rockland Community College… Three Rivers Community College… Daughters of the American Revolution… Civil War Round Tables… Fitch Middle School… Women's Clubs… Genealogical conferences… grammar schools… Connecticut Authors and Publishers Association.

BIBLIOGRAPHY FROM MYSTIC SEAFARER'S TRAIL (INCLUDES AMELIA EARHART SOURCES)

"CAPTAIN NAT". (n.d.). Retrieved September 16, 2012, from Stonington Historical Society Nathaniel B. Palmer House : http://www.stoningtonhistory.org/palmer2.htm

THE BURNED STEAMER: MORE ACCOUNTS OF THE DISASTER. THE DESTRUCTION OF THE CITY OF WACO AT GALVESTON HOPELESS SEARCH FOR THE PASSENGERS AND CREW. CRUISE OF THE BUCKTHORN. FACTS AND CONCLUSIONS. LOCAL COMPANIES. CAPT. THOMAS WOLFE'S BODY TO BE SENT TO CONN. (1875, November 15). *The New York Times.*

THE CITY O THE CITY OF WACO.; THE BODY OF CAPT. WOLFE, THE GALVESTON PILOT, RECOVERED NO HOPE THAT ANY OF THOSE ON BOARD ESCAPED. (1875, November 14). *The New York Times.*

Lucien P. Smith's December Baby. (1912, December 28). *Sphere.* Retrieved September 16, 2012, from http://www.encyclopedia-titanica.org/lucien-p-smiths-december-baby.html

Rescue Ship Arrives—Thousands Gather At the Pier. (1912). *The New York Times.*

"BYRD PLIGHT IS REGARDED AS PERILOUS—Lives May Be Lost if Help Fails To Reach Them—HASTE IS IMPERATIVE—Ice Packs Threaten to Isolate Explorers With Food Supplies Running Low." . (1930, January 24). *Democrat and Chronicle*, pp. 1,20.

AMELIA EARHART WEDS G.P. PUTNAM. (1931, February 8). *The New York Times.*

Certificate of Marriage. (1931, February 7). Retrieved from Pres. Edward Elliot's Residence 1930-1940: http://earchives.lib.purdue.edu/cdm4/document.php?CISOROOT=/earhart&CISOPTR=3003&REC=1

US Army Survival Manual . (1991). New York: Dorset Press .

"The Leaving of Liverpool" Gaelic Mist . (2007, October 15). Retrieved September 16, 2012, from YouTube: http://www.youtube.com/watch?v=bdiLcJ14Mkc

Model 10 Electra. (2012, September 16). Retrieved from Lockheed Martin: http://www.lockheedmartin.com/us/100years/programs/model-10-electra.html

About Us: St. Edmund's Enders Island. (n.d.). Retrieved September 16, 2012, from St. Edmund's Enders Island at Mystic: https://www.endersisland.com/about-us

Lisa Saunders

Adventure Town: Mystic, Conneciticut. (n.d.). Retrieved September 16, 2012, from National Georgraphic: http://adventure.nationalgeographic.com/adventure/trips/adventure-towns/mystic-connecticut/

Mystic River Historical Society. (n.d.). *A Kayakers' Guide to the Mystic River & Its History.* Mystic, Connecticut: Louis Allyn.

AMELIA EARHART BIOGRAPHICAL SKETCH. (n.d.). Retrieved 2012, from Purdue University George Palmer Collections of Amelia Earhart Papers : http://www.lib.purdue.edu/spcol/aearhart/biography.php

Amelia Earhart—An American Hero. (n.d.). Retrieved September 22, 2012, from TheAvWriter: http://youtu.be/Qgk_zvpiIRw

Anderson, Jr., Robert P. (November 17, 2010). *Amelia Earhart in Noank.* Paper given to Ariston Club, New London, and Noank Historical Society. From Noank Historical Society, Inc., Research Files.

BATTISTA, C. (1987, November 01). FOR 'MYSTIC PIZZA,' TOWNS AND RESIDENTS 'JUST ACT NATURAL'. *The New York Times.*

Biography of Amelia Earhart. (n.d.). Retrieved September 16, 2012, from Amelia Earhart Birthplace Museum: http://www.ameliaearhartmuseum.org/AmeliaEarhart/AEBiography.htm

Bonfiglio, A. (2008, October 23-29). Dogs Have Their Day in the Sun. *Rockland County Times.* New York. Retrieved from http://myweb.ecomplanet.com/SAUN6703//Anything%20But%20a%20Dog%21%20Rockland%20County%20Times.pdf

Butler, S. (1999). Amelia Earhart. In *BOOKNOTES: Life Stories, Brian Lamb* (p. 238). New York: Three Rivers Press, Crown Publishing Group, National Cable Satellite Corporation.

Carter, M. W. (1973). *Shipwrecks and Marine Disasters on the Shores of The Town of Westerly, Rhode Island and Adjacent Waters.* Shelter Harbor, Westerly, R.I.: David G. Carter.

Charles C. Sisson Papers (Coll. 114). (n.d.). Retrieved September 16, 2012, from Mystic Seaport: Museum of America and the Sea, Manuscript Collection Registers: http://library.mysticseaport.org/manuscripts/coll/coll114.cfm#restrictlink

Chick, L. (1989, Sept/Oct). Amelia Earhart: The reluctant bride married quietly in Noank. *Tidings,* p. 38, From Noank Historical Society, Inc., Research Files

CLASSIC CUISINE, HISTORIC GOOD TIME . (n.d.). Retrieved September 18, 2012, from Captain Daniel Packer Inne Restaurant and Pub: http://danielpacker.com/history.html

Collette, M. (2010, June 3). Amelia Earhart's connection to Noank commemorated. *The Day*. From Noank Historical Society, Inc., Research Files.

Comrie, M. J. (1981, April 15). *Elm Grove Cemetary Association History*. Retrieved September 16, 2012, from Elm Grove Cemetary: http://elmgrovecemetery.org/history.pdf

Connecticut State Department of Health. (1930, November 8). Marriage License. Groton, Connecticut.

Cutler, C. C. (1930). *Greyhounds of the Sea: The Story of the American Clipper Ship*. G.P. Putnam's Sons.

Denk, R. (1990). *The Complete Sailing Handbook*. London: Tiger Books International PLC.

Descendants of Richard (1608-1684) and Mary (d. 1692) SISSON of Rhode Island, Eight Generation. (n.d.). Retrieved September 19, 2012, from Rootsweb: http://homepages.rootsweb.ancestry.com/~dasisson/richard/aqwg114.htm#32218

Descendants of Richard (1608-1684) and Mary (d. 1692) SISSON of Rhode Island, Ninth Generation. (n.d.). Retrieved September 19, 2012, from Rootsweb: homepages.rootsweb.ancestry.com/~dasisson/richard/aqwg172.htm#32225

Discovering Titanic . (n.d.). Retrieved October 28, 2012, from Mystic Aquarium: http://www.mysticaquarium.org/titanic/860-discovering-titanic

Dorothy Putnam. (n.d.). Retrieved from St. Lucie Historical Society, Inc.: http://martincountydemocr.easycgi.com/stlucie/dorothyputnam.htm

Earhart, A. (1931, February 7). *Letter, 1931 Feb. 7, Noank, Conn., to GPP (draft)*. Retrieved from Pres. Edward Elliot's Residence 1930-1940: http://earchives.lib.purdue.edu/cdm4/document.php?CISOROOT=/earhart&CISOPTR=2999&REC=16

Earhart, A. (n.d.). *Letter_2901 Caption: Letter from Amelia Earhart to Byrd, July 30, 1928, Richard E. Byrd Papers, #2901. Amelia Earhart pledged not only her good wishes, but also money she earned from a cigarette ad, to Byrd's Antarctic Expedition*. Retrieved September 18, 2012, from Ohio State University Libraries, Conquering the Ice: Byrd's Flight to the South Pole: http://library.osu.edu/projects/conquering-the-ice/LETTER_2901.jpg

Encyclopedia Titanic. (n.d.). Lucian Philip Smith. Retrieved from http://www.encyclopedia-titanica.org/titanic-victim/lucian-philip-smith.html

Encyclopedia Titanica. (n.d.). Mary Eloise Smith. Retrieved September 16, 2012, from http://www.encyclopedia-titanica.org/titanic-survivor/mary-eloise-smith.html

Estate of John E. McDonald, D. (1930, May 1). Administrator's Deed. Groton, Connecticut,

United States.

Fagin, S. (1979, February). Spirit of Amelia Earhart still flies high in Noank. *New London Day,* pp. 1,20. From Noank Historical Society, Inc., Research Files.

Flannery, J. (1984, August). Tall Ships sail on in wake of tragedy. *Soundings.*

Fought, L. (2007). *A History of Mystic Connecticut: From Pequot Village to Tourist Town.* Charleston, SC: History Press.

German, A. W. (2005). *Mystic Seaport: A Visitor's Guide.* Mystic, CT: Mystic Seaport.

Ginger Rogers: The Official Site. (n.d.). Retrieved from http://www.gingerrogers.com/about/quotes.html

Goodman, Mary Virginia (circa 1971). *The Groton News, Noank Notes.* Noank, Connecticut. From Noank Historical Society, Inc., Research Files.

Gordinier, G. S. (2012). *The Rockets' Red Glare: The War of 1812 and Connecticut.* New London, CT: New London Historical Society.

Grant, R. (2002). *Flight: 100 Years of Aviation.* New York: DK Publising, Inc.

Grimes, W. (2007, July 20). Beyond 'Moby-Dick': When America Went A-Fishing for the Whale. *The New York Times.*

Hall, N. (1995, March 26). Amelia Earhart grounded long enough to get married in Noank. *Norwich Bulletin.* From Noank Historical Society, Inc., Research Files.

In Memoriam: Drowned off Galveston Bar...Steamer City of Waco...Capt. Thomas Eldredge Wolfe...Inquest. (n.d.). From Mystic River Historical Society.

John Bishop Putnam. (n.d.). Retrieved from wikepedia: http://en.wikipedia.org/wiki/John_Bishop_Putnam

Kimball, C. W. (2002, January 17). Capt. Thomas E. Wolfe of Mystic lived life to the hilt. *The Day.* From Mystic River Historical Socieity.

Kimball, C. W. (2005). *Historic Glimpses: recollections of days past in the Mystic River Valley.* Mystic, Connecticut: Flat Hammock Press.

King, J. (2011, August 31). *Groton Respite Center Wants Town, Region To Take Showers.* Retrieved from Groton Patch: http://groton.patch.com/articles/groton-respite-center-wants-town-region-to-take-showers

King, J. (2011, March 6). *Project Oceanology Seal Cruise (with Video).* Retrieved September 16, 2011, from New London Patch: http://montville-ct.patch.com/articles/project-oceanology-seal-cruise-with-video-3#video-5155164

Leavitt, J. F. (1973). *The Charles W. Morgan.* Mystic, Connecticut: Mystic Seaport, The Marine Historical Association, Incorporated.

Leslie, E. E. (1988). *Desperate Journeys, Abandoned Souls: True stories of casaways and other survivors.* Boston: Houghton Mifflin Company.

Life Book's. (2000). The Greatest Adventures of All Time. Time Inc. Home Entertainment.

Lockett, B. J. (2009). *Mystic Connecticut: A Woman's Hundred Year Journy to Heaven.* Mystic: Life's Journey Publishing Co.

Long, Elgen M. & Marie K. (1999). *Amelia Earhart: The Mystery Solved.* New York: Simon & Schuster.

Marshall, B. T. (1922). *A modern history of New London County, Connecticut.* Lewis Historical Publishing Company.

McDowell, L. R. (2013). *Vitamin History, the early years.* E-book (in press).

McManus, M. M. (2012, July). *Researchers Searching For Amelia Earhart's Plane Wreckage Sail From Hawaii To Nikumaroro.* Retrieved August 2012, from Huffington Post: http://www.huffingtonpost.com/2012/07/03/amelia-earhart-search-hawaii-nikumaroro_n_1648117.html

Melville, H. (1851). *Moby Dick, or, the whale.*

Mercer, K. (2011). *Shari's Pet Sitting Service.* Retrieved September 16, 2012, from MysticShops.TV: http://mysticshops.tv/shari-pet-sitting

Merz, E. (2012, September 5). Communications, Mystic Aquarium. (L. Saunders, Interviewer)

Mill, J. (1976, November 12). Residents recall Earhart Wedding. *THE NEWS.* From Noank Historical Society, Inc., Research Files.

Muttart, Willaim P. & Ashley, Linda R. (2006). *One Hundred & Eleven Questions & Answers Concerning the Pilgrims: Passengers on the Mayflower, 1620.* Montville, CT: Mayflower Books.

Mystic Pizza: 20th Anniversary Movie Trail. (n.d.). Retrieved September 16, 2012, from http://www.mysticchamber.org/doc/1/Mystic%20Pizza%20Movie%20Trail%20-%20Web.pdf

Mystic River Historical Society. (1995). *Curbstones, Clapboards and Cupolas.* Mystic Rivers Historical Society.

Mystic River Historical Society. (2004). *Images of America Mystic .* Arcadia Publishing.

Mystic River Historical Society. (2010). *Colors of Mystic.* Mystic: Mystic River Historical Society.

Mystic River Historical Society. (n.d.). *About Us.* Retrieved September 25, 2012, from Mystic River Historical Society: http://www.mystichistory.org/about_mrhs.htm

Mystic River Historical Society. (n.d.). Mystic River Walking Adventure. Retrieved from www.mystichistory.org/MRHSTourGravelnobg_72dpi.pdf

Nair, M. (Director). (2009). *Amelia* [Motion Picture].

Peterson, W. N. (1989). *"Mystic Built": Ships and Shipyards of the Mystic River, 1784-1919.* . Mystic : Mystic Seaport Museum.

Peterson, W. N. (1998). The Wartime Shipbuilding Boom at Mystic, Connecticut. In W. M. Benjamin W. Labaree, *American and the Sea: A Maritime History* (pp. 358-359). Mystic, CT: Mystic Seaport.

Piven, Joshua & Borgenicht, David. (1999). *The Worst-Case Scenerio Survival Handbook.* Quirk Productions.

Reardon, N. (2010, November 18). Landscape Unlimited, Stonington, CT (client: Elm Grove Cemetary). (L. Saunders, Interviewer)

Records of the bark Marques (Coll. 244). (n.d.). Retrieved September 16, 2012, from Mystic Seaport: The Museum of American and the Sea, Manuscript Collection Registers: http://library.mysticseaport.org/manuscripts/coll/coll244.cfm

Santos, T. (n.d.). *Mystic in the 1950s: Growing Up in a Small Village.*

Saunders, L. (1995). *Ride a Horse Not an Elevator.* Lisa Saunders.

Saunders, L. (2004). *Ever True: A Union Private and His Wife.* Maryland: Heritage Books.

Saunders, L. (2009). *Anything But a Dog! The perfect pet for a girl with congenital CMV (cytomegalovirus).* Unlimited Publishing LLC.

Saunders, L. (2010, December 16). Gloria the goose survives to see another Christmas. *Mystic River Press.*

Saunders, L. (2011, January 4). *Cast Your Vote For The Eighth Wonder Of Mystic.* Retrieved from Stonington-Mystic Patch: http://stonington.patch.com/articles/cast-your-vote-for-the-eighth-wonder-of-mystic

Saunders, L. (2011). *Cindy Modzelewski gives a kayak launching lesson .* Retrieved from YouTube—LisaSaundersCom: http://www.youtube.com/user/LisaSaundersCom?feature=mhee#p/u/5/oQDOq9eiLsw

Saunders, L. (2011, August 5). *Kate and Bailey at Ford's Lobster*. Retrieved October 1, 2012, from YouTube—LisaSaundersCom: http://www.youtube.com/watch?v=iGXAMY65Mi08&list=ULiy?jnwG7JbVj7T3p pPEjqHw&index=4&feature=plcp

Saunders, L. (2011). *Shays' Rebellion: The Hanging of Co-Leader, Captain Henry Gale*. Connecticut: Lisa Saunders.

Saunders, L. (2011). *The 7 Wonders of Mystic—Mystic Pizza and Beyond!* Lisa Saunders.

Scotti, R. (2003). *Sudden Sea: The Great Hurricane of 1938*. Boston, New York, London: Little, Brown and Company.

Shanghai—Definition of. (n.d.). Retrieved October 2, 2012, from oxforddictionaries.com: http://oxforddictionaries.com/definition/american_english/shanghai?region=us &q=shanghaiing

The Earhart Project. (n.d.). Retrieved September 16, 2012, from The International Group for Historic Aircraft Recovery (TIGHAR): http://tighar.org/Projects/Earhart/Archives/Research/Bulletins/63_DebrisField /63_DebrisField.htm

The International Group for Historical Aircraft Recovery. (n.d.). Retrieved August 2012, from TIGHAR: http://tighar.org/

The Morgan in the Movies. (n.d.). Retrieved September 16, 2012, from Mystic Seaport: Museum of America and the Sea: http://www.mysticseaport.org/index.cfm?fuseaction=home.viewPage&page_id= B61320D3-65B8-D398-7A1BB0E4609C4E5C

The Sisson Stones. (n.d.). From Mystic River Historical Society.

Washington Potatoes Are Nutritious. (n.d.). Retrieved September 17, 2012, from Washington State Potatoe Commission: http://potatoes.com/Nutrition.cfm

Waitzkin, B. (1984, August). Tall Ship Tragedy. *Motor Boating & Sailing*, p. 39.

Waterman, C. (2010). *Landmarks You Must Visit In Southeast Connecticut*. Mystic, Connecticut: Matthew Goldman aka Constant Waterman.

Wilson, J. & B. (1982, October-November). Amelia's Last Flight. *Modern Maturity*. From Noank Historical Society, Inc., Research Files.

Young, S. (1970, November 11). Amelia Earhart Made News in Noank. *The Day*, p. 40. From Noank Historical Society, Inc., Research Files.

Interviews

Acas, E. (2010, Fall). Marketing Communications Coordinator; Pelli Clarke Pelli
    Architects. (L. Saunders, Interviewer)

Anderson, J. J. (2010, October 27). Executive Director, St. Edmunds Retreat,
    Enders Island. (L. Saunders, Interviewer)

Anderson, M. (2012, August). Curator, Noank Historical Society. (L. Saunders,
    Interviewer) Noank, Connecticut.

Anderson, Jr., R. P. (2012, September 26). Lawyer. (L. Saunders, Interviewer)

Baker, M. B. (2012, August 29). Director, Stonington Historical Society. (L.
    Saunders, Interviewer)

Blanch, L. M. (2010, 2012). Navy Community Liaison. (L. Saunders, Interviewer)

Bradford, Katie. (2012, September). Owner, Custom Marine Canvas. (L. Saunders,
    Interviewer)

Buffum Jr., C. C. (2012, September 7). Owner, Cottrell Brewing Company. (L.
    Saunders, Interviewer)

Coleman, R. (2010, October 27). Bridgetender, Mystic River Bascule Bridge. (L.
    Saunders, Interviewer)

Davis, J. (FAll 2010). Superintendent, Elm Grove Cemetary. (L. Saunders,
    Interviewer)

Dombrowski, S. (2010, November 12). Hilton. (L. Saunders, Interviewer)

G., S. (2010, November 5). Waitress, Mystic Pizza. (L. Saunders, Interviewer)

Hanna, D. (2012, September 14). Collections Manager, Mystic River Historical
    Society. (L. Saunders, Interviewer)

Peterson, B. (2010, November 17). Mystic Historian. (L. Saunders, Interviewer)

Reed, F. (2012, August 27). Manager of NavList . (L. Saunders, Interviewer)

Robertson, C. (2012, September 4). Olde Mistick Village. (L. Saunders, Interviewer)

Servidio, B. (2012, August 26). (L. Saunders, Interviewer)

Stackpole, M. (2011, November 5). Ship's Historian. (L. Saunders, Interviewer)

Sullivan, B. (. (2010, October 2010). Bridgetender, Mystic River Bascule Bridge. (L.
    Saunders, Interviewer)

Zelepos, J. (2010, November 9). Owner, Mystic Pizza. (L. Saunders, Interviewer)

ENDNOTES

i

http://www.youtube.com/watch?v=r6XAMY65Mi0&list=UUy2jnwG7JbVjzT3ppPEjqHw
&index=4&feature=plcp

ii (Robert P. Anderson, Jr., November 17, 2010)

iii (Dorothy Putnam)

iv (AMELIA EARHART BIOGRAPHICAL SKETCH)

v (Butler, 1999, p. 238)

vi (Long & Long, 1999, p. 37)

[vii] (Chick, 1989, p. 40)

[viii] http://memory.loc.gov/service/mss/eadxmlmss/eadpdfmss/2003/ms003068.pdf
Library of Congress: The papers of Nathaniel Brown Palmer and other family members were deposited in the Library of Congress in several installments between 1927 and 1937 by Elizabeth Dixon (Mrs. Richard Fanning) Loper, Alexander Palmer Loper, and other members of the Loper family. These deposits were later converted to gifts and purchases. Additional papers were Palmer-Loper Family Papers given to the Library by Alexander P. Loper in 1938-1939, and by Harriet B. Brown, Malcolm F. Brown, and Mark Palmer between 1992 and 2000.

[ix] (Long & Long, 1999, p. 40)

[x] (Amelia Earhart--An American Hero)

[xi] (Earhart, Letter_2901 Caption: Letter from Amelia Earhart to Byrd, July 30, 1928, Richard E. Byrd Papers, #2901.)

[xii] (Mill, 1976)

[xiii] (Mill, 1976)

[xiv] (Chick, 1989)

[xv] (Earhart, Letter, 1931 Feb. 7, Noank, Conn., to GPP (draft), 1931)

[xvi] (Mill, 1976)

[xvii] (Robert P. Anderson, Jr., November 17, 2010)

[xviii] (Mill, 1976)

[xix] (Mill, 1976)

[xx] (AMELIA EARHART WEDS G.P. PUTNAM, 1931)

[xxi] (Mill, 1976)

[xxii] (Chick, 1989)

[xxiii] (Mill, 1976)

[xxiv] (Mill, 1976)

[xxv] (Mill, 1976)

[xxvi] (Mary Virginia Goodman, circa 1971)

[xxvii] (AMELIA EARHART WEDS G.P. PUTNAM, 1931)

[xxviii] (Robert P. Anderson, Jr., November 17, 2010)

[xxix] (AMELIA EARHART BIOGRAPHICAL SKETCH)

[xxx] (Life Book's, 2000)

[xxxi] (AMELIA EARHART BIOGRAPHICAL SKETCH)

[xxxii] (Wilson, 1982)

[xxxiii] (Fagin, 1979)

[xxxiv] (Collette, 2010)

[xxxv] (The International Group for Historical Aircraft Recovery)

[xxxvi] (McManus, 2012)

[xxxvii] Lou Allyn was raised in Mystic and attended schools on both sides of the river and retired "back home" to Masons Island in 1998. Mystic and its history has always been a love of his, along with the Great Hurricane of 1938. His family tree includes great grandfather Louis Allyn who built the house on the northeast corner of Allyn Street and New London Road and grandmother Laura Greenman. (He remembers visiting the aunts and uncles at the George Greenman house and marveled that they had a real whaling ship at the end of their vegetable garden.) Lou Allyn is active in the Mystic River Historical Society and several other community organizations in Mystic..

www.ingramcontent.com/pod-product-compliance
Lightning Source LLC
Chambersburg PA
CBHW070950040426
42443CB00012B/3292